# INTRODUCTION

This booklet by the Astronomy Corresponder provides a convenient guide to seeing the stars, The twelve monthly charts on pp.4–26 show those objects above the evening. The charts have been drawn for the latitude of London (51°30' north) but may be used for any part of the British Isles. Opposite each chart are notes on the visibility of the planets and phases of the Moon. Times of sunset, twilight and sunrise are tabulated on page 29 along with notes on the principal meteor showers. Further notes on the more interesting events in 2003 appear on pp.31–32. A detailed explanation of the astronomical terms used and how the various phenomena arise can be found in the fully illustrated *The Times Night Sky Companion*.

## The Changing Aspect of the Night Sky

From our position on the surface of the Earth, the stars appear to lie on the inside of a spherical surface, called the celestial sphere. Because the stars are so far away their directions remain essentially unchanged when seen from different parts of the Earth's orbit. The diagram on the inside cover (*see* left) shows one such direction, indicated by the arrow pointing to the First Point of Aries. The stars that lie behind the Sun as seen from the Earth at the beginning of April each year will, by October, be in the opposite part of the sky to the Sun and be due south at midnight. The arrow points to Pisces (where the First point of Aries now lies) and looking at the October chart Pisces is indeed in the southern sky but it does not appear at all on the April chart, being behind the Sun and in the daytime sky. More generally, a line from the Sun through the position of the Earth points towards the stars seen near the lower centre of the chart for that month. Remembering this, one can relate the positions of the other planets in their orbits to where they will be in the sky, though they will not always be on the monthly chart, being too near to the Sun in direction.

## Time of Observation and Location

Greenwich Mean Time (GMT but also known as Universal Time) is used throughout this booklet. When in force, British Summer Time (BST) is 1 hour ahead of GMT, e.g. 23h BST is 22h GMT. Strictly speaking, the charts are only correct in the stars they show above the horizon for an observer near London (Greenwich). As one moves north fewer stars appear above the southern horizon. Movement east or west along the same latitude does not alter what stars can be seen, but only when they can be seen.

## Using the Charts

The charts show the brighter stars above the horizon for London at 23h (11pm) at the beginning, 22h (10pm) in the middle and 21h (9pm) at the end of each month. The stars rise four minutes earlier each night or two hours earlier each month, being back in their same positions at the same time after a year. Thus, for instance, the aspect of the heavens at 23h on 1 April is the same as on 1 May at 21h or 1 March at 01h. By remembering this rule, the chart applicable to any hour throughout the year may be found. This rule does not apply to the Moon and planets. The charts show the whole sky visible at one time with the zenith, the point directly overhead, at the centre of the chart. Note that the Pole Star (Polaris) occupies the same position on every chart being close to one of the two points around which the whole star sphere appears to revolve. It is easily found in relation to Ursa Major at all times of the year and is useful in defining due north. Ursa Major's seven brightest stars form the Plough. The end two stars (the Pointers) are always in line with Polaris. If the observer faces south with the Pole Star to his back and the appropriate chart held up as one would read the booklet, the constellations depicted above the southern horizon should be to the front, with the eastern aspect to the left and western horizon to the right.

*The Times Night Sky Starfinder* can be set to show the stars above the local horizon for any time of any night of the year. It does not show the positions of the Moon or planets, as these vary from year to year, but these are given on the charts in this booklet.

# Explanatory Notes on Terms Used

**The Moon** – the phase and position are given for about 22h on every other day when it is above the horizon at that time. The average time between like phases (e.g. full to full) is 29.5 days, 2 days longer than it takes to return amongst the same stars. It moves eastwards by its own diameter every hour.

**The Planets** – are shown in the position they occupy about the middle of the month unless otherwise indicated, and for Venus and Mars an arrow shows by its length the movement during the month. Planets crossing the meridian (i.e. due south) before midnight are said to be evening stars while those crossing the meridian after midnight are morning stars. A planet is in opposition to the Sun when it is in the opposite part of the sky to the Sun and therefore due south at midnight. (Mercury and Venus can never be at opposition.) It is then at its closest and brightest for that year. For a few weeks on either side of opposition, motion among the stars, instead of being from west to east as usual, is from east to west and is called retrograde. At the turning points, where motion is reversed, the planet is said to be stationary. A planet coming in line with the Earth and the Sun is said to be in superior conjunction with the Sun if it lies beyond the Sun but at inferior conjunction if it lies between the Earth and the Sun. Only Mercury and Venus can be at inferior conjunction. Planets can also be in conjunction with others when close in the sky. Mercury and Venus are said to be at greatest elongation when at their greatest apparent distance from the Sun, either east (evening) or west (morning). They can never be high in the sky late at night. Mercury is not observable in a dark sky from the British Isles and may require binoculars. It is always too near the sun to be included on the monthly charts. Uranus is visible at times to the naked eye but will probably require binoculars for identification. Neptune always requires optical aid. Pluto requires a moderate-sized telescope and is not mentioned in the monthly notes. Opposition in 2003 is on 9 June, the 14th magnitude planet being in Ophiuchus.

# ECLIPSES AND TRANSIT OF MERCURY

## 7 MAY

Mercury will pass across (transit) the face of the Sun at inferior conjunction on the 7th. This event, which lasts several hours, will be visible from Asia, Australasia, Africa, Europe and the eastern half of the Americas. Viewing the Sun can be extremely dangerous and the same precautions recommended for observing solar eclipses must be taken. See p. 31.

## 16 MAY

This total eclipse of the Moon will be visible over a wide area centred on central S America. As the Moon will pass close to the northern edge of the Earth's umbral shadow, totality will last only 52 minutes. The Moon enters the umbra at 02h 03m and totality begins at 03h 14m, when it will be twilight over much of the British Isles. Mid-eclipse will be at 03h 40m UT.

## 31 MAY

An annular solar eclipse occurs when the Moon appears too small to cover the Sun, even at mid-eclipse and the Sun appears as a bright ring, swamping the faint light of the solar corona visible at a total eclipse. This annular eclipse will be visible from parts of NW Scotland, Orkney and Shetland as well as Iceland and central Greenland. A partial solar eclipse will be seen over parts of Europe, N & W Asia, Alaska and N Canada. Mid-eclipse is about 03h 45m in Scotland and 03h 35m in London. The Sun will be very low, only 2-3 degrees up in Orkney and Shetland, and lower in Scotland so a clear view to the NE horizon is essential. In SW Scotland and the rest of the British Isles the Sun will rise after mid-eclipse and only the later stages of a partial eclipse will be seen low in the NE sky. The next annular eclipse visible from the British Isles is in 2093 and the next total solar eclipse visible from mainland British Isles not until 2090: as in 1999 the path of totality will cross Devon and Cornwall. See p. 31 for further details.

## 8–9 NOVEMBER

In this total eclipse the Moon just dips into the southern part of the umbra so the length of totality is only 24 minutes with mid-eclipse at 01h 18m. The Moon enters the umbra at 23h 32m and leaves at 03h 04m. The total eclipse will be visible from Europe (including the British Isles) , W Africa, the Americas, Greenland and parts of Antarctica.

## 23–24 NOVEMBER

The path of the total phase of this eclipse of the Sun crosses part of Antarctica and a small part of the Southern (Indian) Ocean. A partial eclipse will cover Antarctica, Patagonia, most of Australia and the S island of New Zealand.

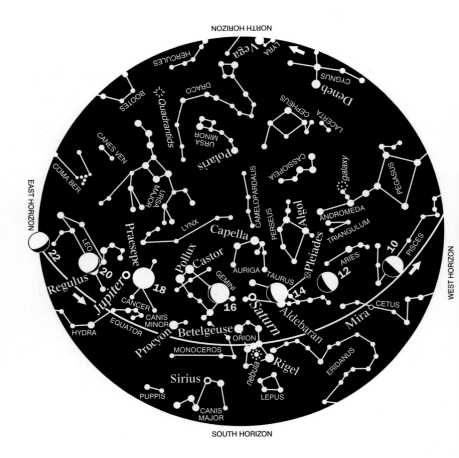

**JANUARY 1, 23h (11pm)**

The aspect of the sky (apart from the Moon and Planets) will be approximately the same in other months at the following times:

**October 1, 05h: November 1, 03h: December 1, 01h: February 1, 21h: March 1, 19h.**

The time in these notes is that of the Greenwich meridian.

# JANUARY

## The Planets

MERCURY is at inferior conjunction on the 11th. By the 31st it may be visible at 0.0 magnitude (mag) in morning twilight low in the SE. Moon to the south on the 30th.

VENUS is -4.5 mag rising 4h before the Sun on the 1st and 3h before by the 31st. It will be at greatest western elongation (47 degrees) on the 11th. Moon nearby on the 28th.

MARS is 1.4 mag and rises about 04h throughout the month. In Libra it passes through Scorpius into Ophiuchus by the 31st. Moon nearby on the 27th, Mars above Venus early in the month and north of Antares on the 31st.

JUPITER is -2.5 mag and in Cancer, being above the horizon all night. Moon nearby on the 18th–19th.

SATURN is -0.3 mag and in Taurus, setting by 05h by the 31st. Moon close by on the 15th.

URANUS passes from Capricornus into Aquarius in late January.

NEPTUNE is in Capricornus throughout the year. It is in conjunction with the Sun on the 31st and not observable.

## The Moon

New Moon 2d 20h
First quarter 10d 13h
Full Moon 18d 11h
Last quarter 25d 09h

The Earth: at perihelion 4d 05h (147 million km)

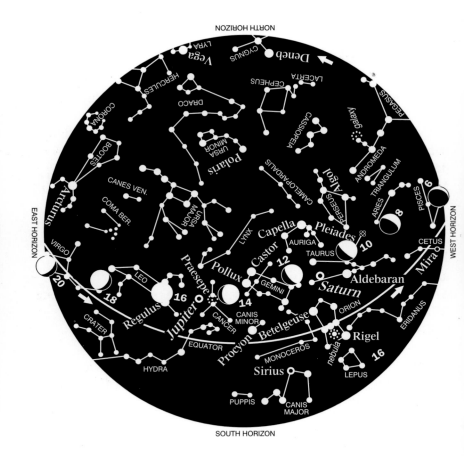

## FEBRUARY 1, 23h (11pm)

The aspect of the sky (apart from the Moon and Planets)
will be approximately the same in other months at the
following times:

**November 1, 05h: December 1, 03h: January 1, 01h:
March 1, 21h: April 1, 19h.**

The time in these notes is that of the Greenwich meridian.

# FEBRUARY

## The Planets

MERCURY reaches greatest western elongation (25 degrees) on the 4th. It may just be visible for the first few days of the month low in the SE before sunrise.

VENUS is a morning star rising less than 2h before the Sun by the 28th. Moon to the south on the 27th.

MARS slowly brightens to 1.1 mag passing into Sagittarius in late February. It rises about 03h 30m. Moon close by on the 25th.

JUPITER is at opposition on the 2nd in Cancer, a conspicuous -2.6 mag. Moon to north on the 15th.

SATURN is -0.1 mag in Taurus, setting by 03h by the 28th. Stationary on the 22nd. Moon to the north on the 11th.

URANUS is in Aquarius but in conjunction with the Sun on the 17th and not observable.

NEPTUNE is in Capricornus rising by 06h on the 28th.

## The Moon

New Moon 1d 11h
First quarter 9d 11h
Full Moon 17d 00h
Last quarter 23d 17h

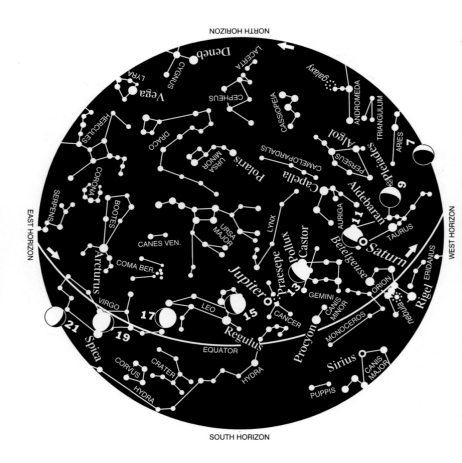

## MARCH 1, 23h (11pm)

The aspect of the sky (apart from the Moon and Planets) will be approximately the same in other months at the following times:

### December 1, 05h: January 1, 03h: February 1, 01h: April 1, 21h.

The time in these notes is that of the Greenwich meridian.

# MARCH

## The Planets

MERCURY is at superior conjunction on the 22nd and then moves into the evening sky to become visible in April. VENUS moves into bright morning twilight by mid-month and will continue to rise only an hour before the Sun until superior conjunction in August. MARS is moving quickly eastwards through Sagittarius, brightening to 0.5 magnitude and rising by 03h by the 31st. Moon nearby on the 25th–26th. JUPITER is in Cancer and -2.4 mag setting by 04h by the 31st. Moon to the north on the 14th. SATURN is in Taurus and 0.0 mag, setting by 01h by the 31st. Moon to the north on the 11th. URANUS rises an hour before the Sun by the 31st. Moon to the south on the 29th. NEPTUNE rises by 04h by the 31st. Moon to the south on the 28th.

## The Moon

New Moon 3d 03h
First quarter 11d 07h
Full Moon 18d 11h
Last quarter 25d 02h

The Earth: Spring Equinox 21d 01h

**APRIL 1, 23h (11pm)**

The aspect of the sky (apart from the Moon and Planets) will be approximately the same in other months at the following times:

**December 1, 07h: January 1, 05h: February 1, 03h: March 1, 01h: May 1, 21h.**

The time in these notes is that of the Greenwich meridian.

# APRIL

## The Planets

MERCURY is a bright -1.4 mag on the 1st fading to 0.0 at greatest eastern elongation (20 degrees) on the 16th when it sets 2h after the Sun. It should be an easy object in the W sky until mid-month. Moon above on the 3rd.

VENUS rises only an hour before the Sun and will be very difficult to observe.

MARS brightens to 0.0 mag by the 30th when it rises by 02h. During April it moves from Sagittarius into Capricornus. Moon to the south on the 23rd.

JUPITER is in Cancer setting by 02h. Stationary on the 4th. Moon nearby on the 10th–11th.

SATURN is in Taurus, setting before midnight by the 30th. Moon to the north on the 7th.

URANUS in Aquarius rises before 03h by the 30th. Moon to the south on the 25th.

NEPTUNE in Capricornus rises by 02h by the 30th. Moon to the south on the 24th.

## The Moon

New Moon 1d 19h
First quarter 10d 00h
Full Moon 16d 20h
Last quarter 23d 12h

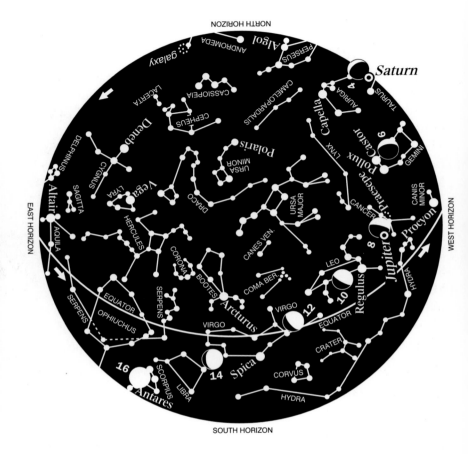

**MAY 1, 23h (11pm)**

The aspect of the sky (apart from the Moon and Planets) will be approximately the same in other months at the following times:

**January 1, 07h: February 1, 05h: March 1, 03h: April 1, 01h: June 1, 21h.**

The time in these notes is that of the Greenwich meridian.

# MAY

## The Planets

MERCURY is at inferior conjunction on the 7th when it transits the face of the Sun.

VENUS remains very low in morning twilight, rising only an hour before the Sun.

MARS is in Capricornus brightening to -0.6 magnitude by the 31st when it rises about 0h 30m. Moon to the south on the 22nd.

JUPITER is -2.0 mag and in Cancer , setting at 0h by the 31st. Moon to the north on the 8th.

SATURN passes from Taurus into northern Orion in mid-May when it sets about 2h after the Sun. Moon nearby on the 4th–5th.

URANUS is in Aquarius rising before 01h by the 31st. Moon to the south on the 22nd–23rd.

NEPTUNE rises about 0h by the 31st. It is stationary on the 16th. Moon to the south on the 21st–22nd.

## The Moon

New Moon 1d 12h
First quarter 9d 12h
Full Moon 16d 04h
Last quarter 23d 01h
New Moon 31d 04h

Transit of Mercury on the 7th and eclipses on the 16th and 31st: *see* p. 3

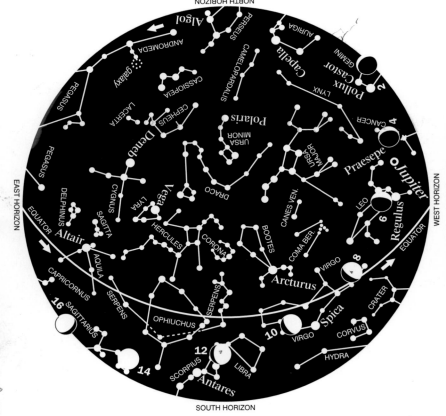

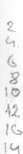

**JUNE 1, 23h (11pm)**

The aspect of the sky (apart from the Moon and Planets)
will be approximately the same in other months at the
following times:

**February 1, 07h: March 1, 05h: April 1, 03h:
May 1, 01h: July 1, 21h.**

The time in these notes is that of the Greenwich meridian.

# JUNE

## The Planets

MERCURY is a morning star at greatest western elongation (24 degrees) on the 3rd but will be in too bright a sky to be seen.
VENUS is also in bright twilight, rising only an hour before the Sun.
MARS passes into Aquarius in early June to end the month a bright -1.4 mag. It rises by 23h on the 30th. Moon to the south on the 19th. Uranus to the north on the 20th.
JUPITER sets about 22h late in the month, moving from Cancer into Leo. Moon to the north on the 5th.
SATURN is in conjunction with the Sun on the 24th.
URANUS is stationary on the 7th. Moon to the south on the 19th.
NEPTUNE rises about 22h by the 30th. Moon to the south on the 18th.

## The Moon

First quarter 7d 20h
Full Moon 14d 11h
Last quarter 21d 15h
New Moon 29d 19h

The Earth: Summer Solstice 21d 19h

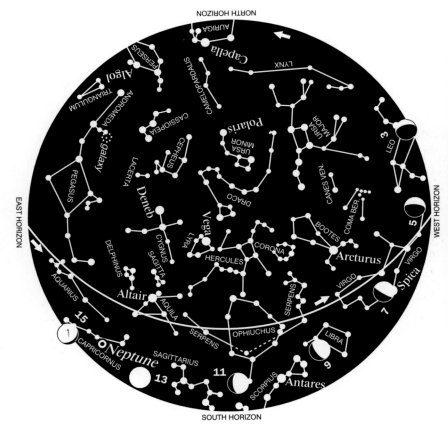

**JULY 1, 23h (11pm)**

The aspect of the sky (apart from the Moon and Planets) will be approximately the same in other months at the following times:

**April 1, 05h: May 1, 03h: June 1, 01h: August 1, 21h: September 1, 19h.**

The time in these notes is that of the Greenwich meridian.

# JULY

## The Planets

MERCURY is at superior conjunction on the 5th becoming an evening object. Setting no more than an hour after the Sun it will not be visible.

VENUS rises only an hour before the Sun and will not be observable.

MARS in Aquarius is a bright -2.3 magnitude by the 31st when it rises about 21h 30m. It is stationary on the 30th and then moves westwards against the stars. Moon nearby on the 16th–17th.

JUPITER is -1.7 mag and in Leo, setting only an hour after the Sun by end-month. Moon to the north on the 2nd an 30th.

SATURN is 0.1 mag and in Gemini. Unobservable until mid-July it will be rising more than 2 hours before the Sun by the 31st. Moon to the north on the 27th.

URANUS is in Aquarius, rising soon after sunset by the 31st. Moon to the south on the 16th–17th.

NEPTUNE is in Capricornus rising at sunset by the 31st. Moon to the south on the 14th.

## The Moon

First quarter 7d 03h
Full Moon 13d 19h
Last quarter 21h 07h
New Moon 29d 07h

The Earth: at aphelion 4d 06h (152 million km)

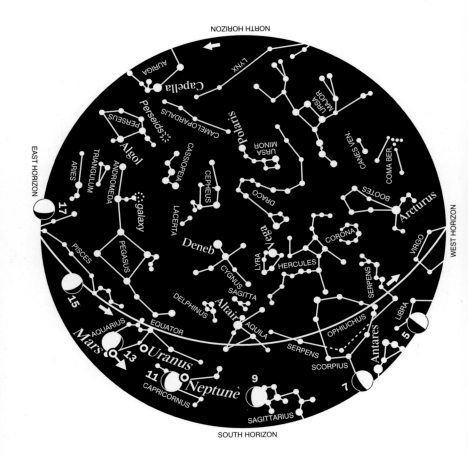

## AUGUST 1, 23h (11pm)

The aspect of the sky (apart from the Moon and Planets) will be approximately the same in other months at the following times:

### June 1, 03h: July 1, 01h: September 1, 21h: October 1, 19h: November 1, 17h.

The time in these notes is that of the Greenwich meridian.

# AUGUST

## The Planets

MERCURY reaches greatest eastern elongation (27 degrees) on the 14th but remains too low after sunset to be seen.

VENUS is at superior conjunction on the 18th, then becoming an evening star but it will not be observable until November.

MARS is a bright -2.8 magnitude retrograding through Aquarius. It will be at opposition on the 28th. Moon close by on the 13th.

JUPITER is in conjunction with the Sun on the 22nd and will not be observable this month.

SATURN is in Gemini rising about 0h by the 31st. Moon to the north on the 23rd.

URANUS is in Aquarius and at opposition on the 24th being above the horizon all night. Moon to the south on the 12th.

NEPTUNE is in Capricornus and at opposition on the 4th. Moon to the south on the 11th.

## The Moon

First quarter 5d 07h
Full Moon 12d 05h
Last quarter 20d 01h
New Moon 27d 17h

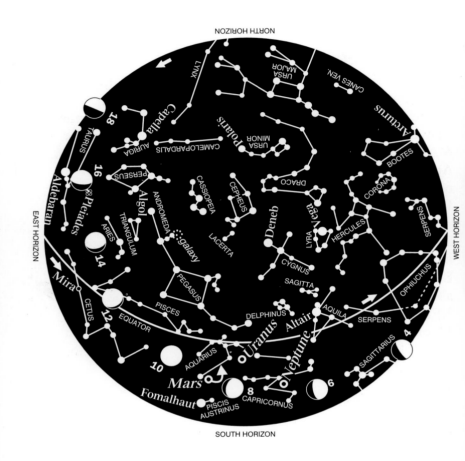

## SEPTEMBER 1, 23h (11pm)

The aspect of the sky (apart from the Moon and Planets) will be approximately the same in other months at the following times:

**July 1, 03h: August 1, 01h: October 1, 21h: November 1, 19h: December 1, 17h.**

The time in these notes is that of the Greenwich meridian.

# SEPTEMBER

## The Planets

MERCURY is at inferior conjunction on the 11th. Reaching greatest western elongation on the 27th (18 degrees) at -0.5 magnitude, it should then be observable in the east, rising 2h before the Sun.

VENUS sets only minutes after the Sun and will not be observable.

MARS is in Aquarius, fading slowly to -2.2 mag by its stationary point on the 29th, when it sets about 02h. Moon nearby on the 8th–9th.

JUPITER is -1.7 mag and in Leo, rising by 03h on the 30th. Moon to the north on the 24th.

SATURN is 0.1 mag and in Gemini, rising soon after 22h by the 30th. Moon to the north on the 20th.

URANUS is in Aquarius setting about 02h 30m by the 30th. Moon to the south on the 8th.

NEPTUNE is in Capricornus setting about 01h by the 30th. Moon to the south on the 7th.

## The Moon

First quarter 3d 13h
Full Moon 10d 17h
Last quarter 18d 19h
New Moon 26d 03h

The Earth: Autumn Equinox 23d 11h

## OCTOBER 1, 23h (11pm)

The aspect of the sky (apart from the Moon and Planets)
will be approximately the same in other months at the
following times:

**August 1, 03h: September 1, 01h: November 1, 21h:
December 1, 19h: January 1, 17h.**

The time in these notes is that of the Greenwich meridian.

# OCTOBER

## The Planets

MERCURY rises 2h before the Sun on the 1st and brightens to -1.2 magnitude as it closes with the Sun to be at superior conjunction on the 25th. Mercury should still be an easy object in the eastern twilight during the first 10 days of October.

VENUS is in the evening sky but is too near the Sun for observation.

MARS is now moving eastwards again through Aquarius fading to -1.3 mag by the 31st. Moon to the south on the 6th.

JUPITER is -1.8 mag and in Leo rising before 02h by the 31st. Moon nearby on the 22nd.

SATURN is 0.0 mag and in Gemini rising about 20h by the 31st. Stationary on the 26th. Moon to the north on the 16th–17th.

URANUS is in Aquarius setting about 0h 30m by the 31st. Moon to the south on the 6th.

NEPTUNE is in Capricornus setting about 22h 30m by the 31st. Stationary on the 23rd. Moon to the south on the 4th and 31st.

## The Moon

First quarter 2d 19h
Full Moon 10d 07h
Last quarter 18d 13h
New Moon 25d 13h

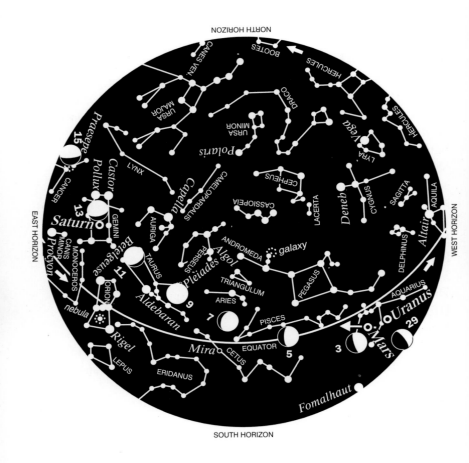

## NOVEMBER 1, 23h (11pm)

The aspect of the sky (apart from the Moon and Planets) will be approximately the same in other months at the following times:

**September 1, 03h: October 1, 01h: December 1, 21h: January 1, 19h: February 1, 17h.**

The time in these notes is that of the Greenwich meridian.

# NOVEMBER

## The Planets

MERCURY is in the evening sky but remains too low for observation.

VENUS at -3.9 magnitude should be visible low in the SW after sunset, becoming more conspicuous in December. Moon below on the 25th.

MARS is in Aquarius fading to -0.5 mag by the 30th when it sets soon after 0h. Moon to the south on the 3rd.

JUPITER is in Leo rising by 0h by the 30th. Moon to the north on the 18th.

SATURN is -0.2 mag and in Gemini rising by 18h on the 30th. Moon to the north on the 13th.

URANUS is in Aquarius, stationary on the 8th and setting by 22h 30m by the 30th. Moon to the south on the 2nd and 29th.

NEPTUNE is in Capricornus, setting about 21h by the 30th. Moon to the south on the 1st and 28th.

## The Moon

First quarter 1d 04h
Full Moon 9d 01h
Last quarter 17d 04h
New Moon 23d 23h
First quarter 30d 17h

Eclipses on the 9th and 23rd: *see* p. 3

## DECEMBER 1, 23h (11pm)

The aspect of the sky (apart from the Moon and Planets)
will be approximately the same in other months at the
following times:

**September 1, 05h: October 1, 03h: November 1, 01h:
January 1, 21h: February 1, 19h.**

The time in these notes is that of the Greenwich meridian.

# DECEMBER

## The Planets

MERCURY is an evening object at greatest eastern elongation (21 degrees) on the 9th but as it sets at most an hour after the Sun it will probably not be visible. It comes to inferior conjunction on the 27th, moving into the morning sky. Moon and Jupiter above on the 24th.

VENUS is -4.0 magnitude and by the 25th will set 2h 30m after the Sun to be a brilliant evening star into the New Year. Moon to the south on the 25th.

MARS moves from Aquarius into Pisces, fading to 0.1 mag by the 31st. Moon to the south on the 1st and 29th.

JUPITER is -2.2 mag and in Leo rising by 22h on the 31st. Moon to the north on the 16th.

SATURN is -0.4 mag and comes to opposition in Gemini on the 31st when it will be above the horizon all night. Moon to the north on the 10th.

URANUS is in Aquarius setting about 20h by the 31st. Moon nearby on the 26th–27th.

NEPTUNE is in Capricornus setting about 19h by the 31st. Moon to the south on the 25th–26th.

## The Moon

Full Moon 8d 21h
Last quarter 16d 18h
New Moon 23d 10h
First quarter 30d 10h

The Earth: Winter Solstice 22d 07h

# THE STARS

The stars are subdivided into magnitudes according to apparent brightness; the lower the number the brighter the star and the larger the dots on our monthly maps. Any star is about 2½ times as bright as one of the next magnitude. The faintest star ordinarily visible to the naked eye is of the 6th magnitude, or just one-hundredth of the brightness of one of the 1st, but that is possible only under a very clear sky. On a moonless night the total number of stars so visible is about 1,000. The faintest object detected with ground-based telescopes is of the 28th magnitude though the Hubble Space Telescope has now reached 30th magnitude.

Zero magnitude (0.0) represents a brightness 2½ times that of a standard first-magnitude star. Brightnesses in excess of this are indicated by a minus sign, the magnitude of Sirius, for example, being -1.47. Venus at its brightest is -4.6 or 145 times as bright as a first-magnitude star. The magnitude of the Full Moon is -12.5, equal to 250,000 first-magnitude stars. The stellar magnitude of the Sun is -26.6 or some 444,000 Full Moons.

The colours of the stars are indications of their surface temperatures. The temperature of a reddish star like Antares is about 3,000°C, and that of a bluish-white star, such as Vega, is about 11,000°C. The temperatures of orange, yellow and white stars are intermediate between these extremes.

An examination of the sky on a clear dark night shows that the distribution of stars is far from uniform. While there are distinct clusters of stars, such as the Pleiades and Praesepe, many other groupings consist of stars that just happen to lie in the same direction but at very different distances. The most noticeable concentration of stars is towards what we call the Milky Way, the faint band of light that passes through the following constellations: Puppis, Monoceros, Gemini, Auriga, Perseus, Cassiopeia, Cepheus, Cygnus, Aquila and Sagittarius. Not all of these constellations are above the horizon at any one time. The band of the Milky Way actually extends right round the sky passing through some southern constellations that never rise above the horizon in the British Isles.

Even binoculars show that the Milky Way is made up of thousands of stars, too faint to be seen with the naked eye. Our Sun is situated well away from the centre of a huge, flattened, disc-like system of stars 100,000 light years across called the Galaxy. It contains more than 100,000 million stars. When we look along the plane of the disc we see the star-clouds of the Milky Way; but when we look out above or below the plane we see far fewer stars.

From a distance, the Galaxy would look like that in Andromeda, visible to the naked eye only as a hazy oval patch of light. This is one of the nearer galaxies, only two-million light years away. Others have been found in their millions; some may be farther than 10,000 million light years distant, each containing thousands of millions of stars. The central bulge of our Galaxy lies towards the great star clouds in Sagittarius, not easily seen from our latitudes.

# SUNSET, SUNRISE AND NAUTICAL TWILIGHT

| Date | | London Area | | | | Edinburgh Area | | | |
|---|---|---|---|---|---|---|---|---|---|
| | | Sunset | End NT | Begin NT | Sunrise | Sunset | End NT | Begin NT | Sunrise |
| Jan | 1 | 16 00 | 17 20 | 06 45 | 08 08 | 15 45 | 17 22 | 07 08 | 08 44 |
| | 15 | 16 20 | 17 40 | 06 40 | 08 00 | 16 10 | 17 43 | 07 00 | 08 45 |
| Feb | 1 | 16 45 | 18 05 | 06 25 | 07 40 | 16 41 | 18 10 | 06 40 | 08 10 |
| | 15 | 17 15 | 18 30 | 06 00 | 07 15 | 17 16 | 18 38 | 06 15 | 07 38 |
| Mar | 1 | 17 35 | 18 50 | 05 35 | 06 50 | 17 47 | 19 05 | 05 40 | 07 03 |
| | 15 | 18 05 | 19 15 | 05 00 | 06 15 | 18 15 | 19 35 | 05 05 | 06 28 |
| Apr | 1 | 18 35 | 19 50 | 04 20 | 05 35 | 18 49 | 20 12 | 04 20 | 05 45 |
| | 15 | 19 00 | 20 10 | 03 40 | 05 00 | 19 20 | 20 52 | 03 45 | 05 05 |
| May | 1 | 19 25 | 20 50 | 03 05 | 04 30 | 19 50 | 21 35 | 02 45 | 04 25 |
| | 15 | 19 45 | 21 35 | 02 30 | 04 05 | 20 15 | 22 25 | 01 56 | 03 47 |
| Jun | 1 | 20 10 | 22 00 | 01 55 | 03 50 | 20 43 | 23 53 | 00 35 | 03 34 |
| | 15 | 20 20 | 22 29 | 01 33 | 03 40 | 21 00 | ----- | ----- | 03 25 |
| Jul | 1 | 20 25 | 22 25 | 01 40 | 03 45 | 21 01 | ----- | ----- | 03 31 |
| | 15 | 20 10 | 22 00 | 02 05 | 04 00 | 20 45 | 23 40 | 00 45 | 03 45 |
| Aug | 1 | 19 50 | 21 30 | 02 40 | 04 20 | 20 19 | 22 22 | 02 10 | 04 15 |
| | 15 | 19 25 | 20 50 | 03 15 | 04 45 | 19 50 | 21 30 | 03 00 | 04 42 |
| Sep | 1 | 18 50 | 20 10 | 03 50 | 05 10 | 19 09 | 20 42 | 03 45 | 05 15 |
| | 15 | 18 15 | 19 30 | 04 20 | 05 35 | 18 30 | 19 52 | 04 20 | 05 43 |
| Oct | 1 | 17 40 | 18 50 | 04 45 | 06 00 | 17 47 | 19 07 | 04 55 | 06 15 |
| | 15 | 17 05 | 18 20 | 05 10 | 06 25 | 17 05 | 18 32 | 05 25 | 06 40 |
| Nov | 1 | 16 35 | 17 50 | 05 40 | 06 50 | 16 31 | 17 57 | 05 52 | 07 19 |
| | 15 | 16 10 | 17 25 | 06 02 | 07 20 | 16 04 | 17 30 | 06 22 | 07 48 |
| Dec | 1 | 15 50 | 17 15 | 06 25 | 07 45 | 15 42 | 17 16 | 06 45 | 08 20 |
| | 15 | 15 50 | 17 13 | 06 37 | 08 03 | 15 36 | 17 10 | 07 00 | 08 38 |
| | 31 | 16 00 | 17 20 | 06 45 | 08 08 | 15 45 | 17 22 | 07 08 | 08 44 |

Times in UT. Also see notes overpage

Notes:

1 Times are given in Universal Time (=GMT): when British Summer Time (BST) is in force (usually from the late March to late October) add 1 hour.

2 Nautical Twilight ends when the Sun's true centre reaches a depression of 12 degrees below the horizon. Then it is dark enough to see the brighter stars and planets, and in suburban areas it often gets no darker due to artificial lighting. Nautical twilight begins when it is becoming too light to see these stars. When no time is shown nautical twilight lasts all night.

3 Times given are approximate and depend on the observer's latitude and longitude. Sunset, sunrise and twilight times will be 4 minutes earlier for every degree of longitude east of the Greenwich meridian and 4 minutes later for every degree west. London is on the Greenwich meridian; Edinburgh is about 3 degrees west or 12 minutes later.

4 The observer's latitude also affects these times: for example sunset occurs earlier in Edinburgh than London in winter but later in summer. It is not possible to cover more than two regions here, but a reasonable estimate can be made for other parts of the British Isles. The times may be used for any year.

# PRINCIPAL METEOR SHOWERS IN 2003

| Name | Period of max. visibility | Av. hourly rate | Visibility and moonlight |
|------|---------------------------|-----------------|--------------------------|
| Quadrantids | 2–4 Jan | 10 | Favourable. New on 2nd. Radiant low in N in eve. |
| Lyrids | 21–22 Apr | 10 | Good before midnight. LQ on 23rd. |
| Perseids | 11–14 Aug | 60 | Unfavourable. Full on 12th |
| Orionids | 20–22 Oct | 10–20 | Favourable. LQ on 18th. |
| Taurids | Late Oct–late Nov | 5–10 | Slow meteors from below Pleiades |
| Leonids | 16–18 Nov | ?? | Strong shower still poss. Rather poor, LQ on 17th |
| Geminids | 12–14 Dec | 60 | Unfavourable. LQ on 16th |

Notes: The Leonids are normally a weak shower but every 33 years activity increases when the parent comet Tempel-Tuttle is near the Sun. Then high but usually short-lived activity may be seen as in the display of fireballs in 1998 and high rates of fainter meteors in 1999, 2000 and 2001. The radiant, from where the meteors appear to come, is from within the 'sickle' reversed question mark) of Leo (major): *see* the December chart. The probability of another very strong shower must now be decreasing, though cannot be ruled out. The last quarter Moon will hinder the observation of any fainter meteors.

Moonlight between first quarter and last quarter interferes with the number of faint meteors seen. Fewer meteors are usually seen when the radiant area is low near the horizon. Radiant areas are shown on the monthly charts, except for the Taurids which covers a wide area and the Leonids which has not risen at the time of the November chart.

# Further Events in 2003

The monthly notes give the magnitudes of the planets as a guide as to how bright they will appear. Venus and Jupiter are always so bright that they are easily identified but Mars and Saturn may be confused with nearby bright stars. Mercury is visible only in twilight. The following easily found bright stars, spread throughout the year, may help to identify the planets by comparing their brightness (magnitude): Polaris (2.0), Aldebaran (0.9), Sirius (-1.5), Castor (1.6), Procyon (0.4), Regulus (1.3), Arcturus (0.0), Spica (1.0) and Altair (0.8). (See p. 28 for an explanation of magnitudes.) For morning events the beginning of nautical twilight (BNT) is a guide as to when it becomes too light to see all but the brightest objects. The end of nautical twilight (ENT) in the evening is about the time when the observation of fainter objects can begin.

The outer planets move more slowly than the Earth and have larger orbits so they all take longer than a year to orbit the Sun. Mars takes 1.9 years, Jupiter 12, Saturn 29.5, Uranus 84 and Neptune 165 years. So Jupiter moves eastwards against the stars by 30 degrees each year while Saturn moves only 12 degrees. Saturn will stay over twice as long as Jupiter in any constellation. While Mars is making one orbit of the Sun, the Earth will have made nearly two and it will be 2 years and 2 months before the planets again line up with the Sun and Mars again comes to opposition. After opposition Mars remains in the evening sky for many months, setting about the same interval after sunset, until eventually it is overtaken by the Sun and is lost in evening twilight. So we get to see Mars well every two years for a few weeks and when it is near opposition it can rival Jupiter in brightness.

The inner planets Mercury and Venus also move eastwards with the Sun but swing to the east and west of the Sun as they become evening or morning objects. Mercury takes 88 days to orbit the Sun and Venus 225 days but their movements are more complicated as being in orbits smaller than that of the Earth, they can never appear to us to be very far from the Sun, for Mercury the maximum angular elongation is 28 degrees and for Venus 47 degrees. In a year Mercury usually has three morning apparitions with another three in the evening. Generally only one or two are favourable to observers at our latitude. Venus takes 19 months from one superior conjunction to the next. More information on the planets and their movements (and other naked eye phenomena) can be found in *The Times Night Sky Companion*.

## Opposition of Mars

Mars has a diameter of 6,800 km, about half the size of the Earth (12,760 km). Mars moves in a more elliptical orbit than the Earth so that its minimum distance from the Sun can range from 208 million km at perihelion to 248 million km at aphelion. The closest approaches to the Earth occur when Mars is both at perihelion and opposition about the same date. Then its distance from the Earth can be as little as 56 million km. When opposition occurs with Mars at aphelion the opposition distance increases to 100 million km. Through a telescope Mars appears nearly twice as large at perihelic oppositions than at aphelic oppositions. Unfortunately for northern observers, perihelic oppositions occur in August and always put the planet well south of the equator and rather low in our sky. A winter opposition puts Mars higher in our sky but being farther from the Sun and Earth it will appear smaller, showing less detail.

This year Mars will be at opposition on 28th August in Aquarius when it will be only 56 million km from the Earth and will show a disc 25.1 seconds of arc across. This is close to the largest it can ever appear, and in a telescope with a magnification of 75 times it will appear as large as the full Moon does to the naked eye. Mars starts the year 310 million km from us, only 4.5 seconds of arc across and +1.6 magnitude. By opposition Mars will have brightened 50 times to reach -2.9 magnitude, as bright as Jupiter, but will fade to 0 mag by December.

Even to the naked eye Mars will become a striking object in the summer and autumn sky, easily identifiable by its reddish colour in an area rather poor in bright stars. Do take the opportunity to see it through a telescope: Mars will not be as close again for 15 years.

## Transit of Mercury

As Mercury and Venus orbit the Sun they occasionally pass directly between the Earth and Sun. Then we have a Transit of Mercury or Venus. The tilt of their orbits relative to the Earth's prevents this from happening at every inferior conjunction.

Transits of Venus are rare, taking place at over hundred year intervals, usually in pairs. Recent events were in 1761 and 1769, and in 1874 and 1882. There will be a transit of Venus on 8 June 2004 wholly visible from the British Isles (see The Times Night Sky 2004) and the later stages of the June 2012 transit will also be visible. After that we must wait for the 2117 and 2125 transits.

Transits of Mercury are more frequent and take place in May and November. Recent events include Nov 1986, Nov 1993 and Nov 1999. The transit this year is on 7 May 2003 and (like the 2004 Transit of Venus) will start in the early morning, which may give a better chance of clear skies in late spring or early summer.

Mercury will be about 84 million km from us and will appear very small (only 12 arc seconds) and will not be visible on the Sun with the naked eye (see below). But if a small telescope of 2 inch (50mm) aperture or more is used to project a 6 inch (153mm) diameter image, Mercury would be seen as a small black dot about 1mm across. Care should be taken not to overheat the optics by continuous exposure to the Sun.

The planet will begin to encroach on the upper left-hand side of the Sun's disc about 05h 00m (6 am BST) and will move slowly across the upper part of the Sun's disc from left to right, leaving the disc about 10h 45m (11h 45m BST).

It must be emphasised that observing the Sun directly is extremely dangerous and can lead to blindness. It is safe to project the Sun's image by means of a small telescope onto a white card to observe the May eclipse or the transit of Mercury but ensure that no one looks through the telescope, finder, binoculars or camera viewfinders, or stares at the Sun with the unprotected eye. Mercury will not be visible using the special dark spectacles designed for observing eclipses, being too small. Direct viewing of the Sun with a telescope or binoculars requires special filters that are expensive and must be supplied by a reputable dealer and demonstrated by an experienced solar observer. Further information on transits, eclipses and how to view them safely can be found in *The Times Night Sky Companion*.